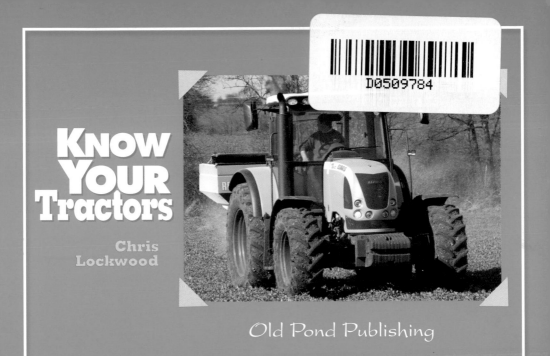

KNOW YOUR Tractors

Chris Lockwood

Old Pond Publishing

First published 2008, reprinted 2008 2009, 2010

ISBN 978-1-905523-91-7

Published by
Old Pond Publishing Ltd
Dencora Business Centre
36 White House Road
Ipswich IP1 5LT
United Kingdom

www.oldpond.com

Book design by Liz Whatling
Printed and bound in China

Contents

Acknowledgements

The photographs are all from my own collection (www.midsuffolkagriphotos.co.uk).
I have gathered
the specifications and information from the manufacturers' own sales literature and websites.

Front cover: An impressive Massey Ferguson 6499, the largest model in
Massey Ferguson's 6400 series, is seen ploughing-under maize stubble.

Title page: Top dressing oilseed rape with a Claas Ares 697 ATZ and
Reco Sulky DPX2004 fertiliser spreader.

Author's Note

Manufacturers' names are included for identification purposes only.

All information and technical specifications are taken from manufacturers' own
sales literature and websites, given in good faith and should only be used as a guide.
The author cannot be held responsible for any errors.

Horsepower figures are given, wherever possible, as rated engine power,
although other measurements may be used occasionally.

Foreword

My aim in this book is to show popular tractor makes and models which are likely to be seen working in fields in every day situations.

In general I have featured modern tractors, and have shown more than one model from the most widely seen makes.

I have also tried to show the tractors carrying out a wide range of tasks, to give a broad perspective of what can be seen going on in fields today.

Many tractor manufacturers are owned by parent companies, some of which own a number of tractor makers. Due to this shared ownership, tractors have many features and components in common.

I thought it would be interesting to include the parent companies of each make to show who owns whom.

I have also included the country of assembly, as different ranges from the same manufacturer are often built in different countries.

Some technical specifications such as power outputs are included, to make it possible to roughly compare different tractors and give an idea of size.

CHRIS LOCKWOOD
Suffolk, 2008

Description

Case IH MXU130X

Assembled and/or manufactured in:
Austria

Parent company:
CNH (Case New Holland)

The MXU130X from Case IH was the largest in the company's MXU Maxxum X Line range of four models spanning 101 to 131hp.

The X Line tractors are intended to be straight forward to operate and are also available with a lower profile version of the Surround Vision cab, which makes them ideal for work in and around buildings.

This example is seen spraying winter beans with an Allman De Luxe 1200l sprayer.

The MXU prefix has recently been dropped on the latest Maxxum X Line range, which now goes up to 141hp.

Description

Case IH MX285

The MX285, with a rated power of 315hp, was top of the MX Magnum series and the largest rigid Case IH tractor when it was launched in 2002. The range also included the smaller MX255 and MX230 models and was aimed at large arable farms.

This MX285 is shown working with a 3 metre wide Simba Solo disc cultivator, aiming to produce seedbeds from stubble in just one pass, the stubble here being from an oilseed rape crop.

More recently the Magnum series has replaced the MX Magnums, and now offers five models rated 224-335hp.

Assembled and/or manufactured in:
USA

Parent company:
CNH (Case New Holland)

Description

Case IH STX450 Quadtrac

Assembled and/or manufactured in:
USA

Parent company:
CNH (Case New Holland)

Along with the other models in the STX Steiger range, the 450 hp STX450 was offered by Case IH in two variants: wheeled, or Quadtrac as shown here.

The Quadtrac design was first introduced in 1996 and has many advantages including lower soil compaction, a smoother ride, and ideal weight distribution when under full load.

Sandy soil is being turned over by this STX450 Quadtrac with the aid of a 12-furrow Grégoire Besson plough.

Currently, the latest Quadtrac range includes four models of 394-548hp, while the wheeled Steiger models start at 394hp and go up to 444hp.

Caterpillar Challenger 55

Assembled and/or manufactured in:
USA

Parent company:
Challenger tractors are now produced by AGCO

Description

The Challenger rubber-tracked crawler tractor was first introduced by Caterpillar in 1987. One of the main advantages of using rubber tracks instead of steel tracks was that the tractor was able to travel on roads without damaging them. Rubber tracks also provided a smoother ride with fewer vibrations.

The 55 was the largest in Caterpillar's 212-270hp range of Challenger tractors, which shared some features with certain New Holland and Fiatagri wheeled tractors.

The 55 seen here is turning in oilseed rape stubble with a six-furrow, French-built Grégoire Besson plough.

Challenger MT765B

Assembled and/or manufactured in:
USA

Parent company:
AGCO

Description

In 2002 AGCO took over the production of Caterpillar Challenger tractors, which they have developed into the current Challenger MT700B and MT800B series.

The MT700B series includes three models, the MT765B being the largest with a 320hp Caterpillar engine.

This MT765B is seen with a Sumo Trailed Trio one-pass cultivator, which is designed and built in England. The tractor is fitted with Challenger's Auto-Guide satellite navigation system which automatically steers the tractor to run straight and ensure that overlaps and underlaps are minimal.

Challenger MT855B

Assembled and/or manufactured in:
USA

Parent company:
AGCO

Description

Carrying on from the MT700B series, the five-model MT800B series starts at 350hp and goes up to a huge 570hp.

Sitting in the middle of the range is the MT855B, with a 15.2 litre 460hp unit under the bonnet which can be useful when working with large trailed machinery such as the Väderstad Rapid A 800 S drill, shown here sowing vining peas grown for canning.

Description

Claas Ares 697 ATZ

Assembled and/or manufactured in:
France

Parent company:
Claas

Claas purchased Renault Agriculture in 2003 and since then has developed the tractors further under their own name, resulting in some new ranges.

The three-model Ares 600 range features ATZ cab suspension as standard, and spans 110-140hp.

A five-furrow Överum Xcelsior DX plough from Sweden is seen being pulled by an Ares 697 ATZ, the largest model in the range.

Claas has recently introduced the new Arion 500 and 600 series tractors, which will ultimately replace the Ares 600 machines.

Description

Claas Challenger 95 E

Assembled and/or manufactured in:
USA

Parent company:
Claas

A joint venture between Caterpillar and Claas to market Challenger tractors in Claas colours in Europe was agreed in 1999.

Two ranges were offered in the lime green livery: the smaller 35, 45, and 55, which all shared the large rear drive wheel layout, and the more powerful Challenger E series tractors.

With 410hp, the largest model offered was the Challenger 95 E, shown here working with a 10-furrow Dowdeswell plough, burying manure.

David Brown 1490

Assembled and/or manufactured in:
UK

Tractors no longer produced

Description

Although David Brown tractors are no longer available new, there are still quite a few to be found earning their keep.

The last tractors to bear the David Brown name were the 90 series models, which included the 83hp 1490, powered by a 4-cylinder turbocharged unit.

This example is seen baling hay with a New Holland 945 baler, towing a Cook flat 8 bale sledge.

In the mid 1980s, with the introduction of the 94 series, the name on the tractors was changed to Case, both companies being owned by Tenneco at the time.

Deutz-Fahr Agrotron 6.00 S

Assembled and/or manufactured in:

Germany

Parent company:
SDF (Same Deutz-Fahr) Group

Description

The innovative, rounded styling of Deutz-Fahr's Agrotron tractors set them apart from other offerings on the market when they were launched in 1995.

The initial line-up consisted of two ranges: the smaller four-cylinders which covered 68-95hp, and the larger six-cylinder tractors which started at 95hp and went up to 145hp.

Here an example of the smallest six-cylinder Agrotron, the 95hp 6.00 S, is shown ploughing light land with a Rabewerk four-furrow plough in preparation for sugar beet.

Deutz-Fahr Agrotron 165 MK3

Assembled and/or manufactured in:
Germany

Parent company:
SDF (Same Deutz-Fahr) Group

Description

In 1995, the Italian Same-Lamborghini-Hürlimann (SLH) Group acquired Deutz-Fahr, the agricultural machinery division of the former Klöckner-Humboldt-Deutz AG, leading to SLH being re-named the Same Deutz-Fahr (SDF) Group.

By the new millennium new and improved Agrotrons were being produced: the Agrotron MK3 series.

Here an Agrotron 165 MK3 is seen with an impressive set-up of front-mounted Sumo FDU (Front Disc Unit) and rear-mounted Sumo Trio, which consists of subsoiler legs, discs, and packer, working land ready for a root crop.

Fendt Favorit 512 C

Assembled and/or manufactured in:

Germany

Parent company:

AGCO

Description

The Favorit 500 C series of tractors from Fendt was made up of six models spanning 95-150hp.

The Favorit 512 C had an MWM engine under the bonnet which produced 125hp. Usually Fendt tractors would have red wheels, rather than the white ones on this Favorit 512 C, seen with an empty Easterby ET 14 trailer whilst carting red onions.

Replacing the Favorit 500 C series were the Farmer 400 Vario and Favorit 700 Vario ranges, both of which used Fendt's revolutionary Vario continuously variable transmission (CVT), allowing stepless speed changes.

Fendt 716 Vario TMS

Assembled and/or manufactured in:
Germany

Parent company:
AGCO

Description

Fendt's 700 Vario range is the third generation of 700 Vario series tractors, and now ranges from 132hp to 181hp. The TMS tractor management system can be fitted so that when activated the tractor's electronics control the engine and transmission, the driver only needing to set the desired speed.

The 716 Vario TMS gets its power from a 165hp Deutz engine, and is seen putting it to good use pulling a five-furrow Kverneland plough to prepare land for winter wheat.

Description

Fiat 880-5 DT

Assembled and/or manufactured in:
Italy

Tractors no longer produced

Fiat's offering for the early 1980s was the 80 series, including the 58hp 580, up to the 180hp 1880.

The 88hp 880-5 was the only tractor in the range which employed a five-cylinder engine as opposed to the more common four or six cylinder. In this case the four-wheel drive DT version is seen ripping up tramlines with a Blyth heavy cultivator.

In 1991 Fiat acquired Ford New Holland and merged it with its own agricultural and earthmoving machinery sector, FiatGeotech, to form N.H. Geotech and later New Holland. Case IH was acquired in 1999, and merged with New Holland to form CNH.

Description

Ford 8210 Generation III

Assembled and/or manufactured in:
UK

Tractors no longer produced

The third generation of 10 series tractors from Ford built on the tradition and reputation of the earlier versions, and included models ranging from 54hp to 110hp.

The largest model in the Generation III range was the 6-cylinder 110hp 8210, an example of which is seen here with a John Deere 550 round baler, stopped when baling winter barley straw.

Although the 10 series finally came to an end in the early 1990s with the introduction of Ford's 40 series tractors, many are still in use today.

Description

Hürlimann Master H-6165

Assembled and/or manufactured in:
Italy

Parent company:
SDF (Same Deutz-Fahr) Group

Hürlimann tractors, originally from Switzerland, have long been associated with Italian manufacturers Same and Lamborghini since they became part of the former Same Group in 1977, leading to the company being re-named the Same – Lamborghini - Hurlimann (SLH) Group.

Consequently the three tractor brands shared many common components although Hürlimann tractors tended to use water-cooled engines rather than the predominantly air-cooled units traditionally used in the Same and Lamborghini machines.

The Master series shared many components with the Lamborghini Racing range. The H-6165 was the middle model, producing 163hp. Recently the green livery has been replaced by silver.

International 1255XL

Assembled and/or manufactured in:

Germany

Name replaced by
Case International

Description

The largest European-built tractors in International's early 1980s range were in the 55 series, the flagship of the range being the 145hp 1455XL.

The smaller sibling of the 1455XL was the 125hp 1255 XL, an example of which is seen here in charge of a trailer holding bags of winter wheat seed.

During the mid 1980s Case acquired International Harvester's agricultural operations through its parent company Tenneco, and the resulting Case IH name was subsequently applied to all future tractors.

Description

JCB Fastrac 2155

Assembled and/or manufactured in:
UK

Parent company:
JCB

When it was launched in the early 1990s the JCB Fastrac was certainly a special machine, being as capable in the field as a conventional tractor, yet able to travel up to 50mph on the road.

The current range is made up of five models, the flagship being the 260hp 8250.

The 160hp Fastrac 2155 (shown) is currently the smallest available, and can travel at a top speed of 37 mph on the road.

A combination of Rabe Combi-Digger subsoiler and Field-Bird disc tiller is seen behind this example.

JCB Fastrac 3190 Plus

Assembled and/or manufactured in:
UK

Parent company:
JCB

Description

Fastracs are ideally suited to a variety of high-speed tasks such as carting grain and straw, as well as being capable of field work like ploughing.

Here a 193hp Fastrac 3190 Plus is shown collecting wheat straw bales with a Walton Eclipse 5666 bale chaser which can pick up individual bales while on the move and later stack them at the edge of the field, or wherever they may be needed.

The Fastrac 3200, also 193hp, has now replaced the 3190 in the current line-up.

John Deere 6820

Assembled and/or manufactured in:
Germany

Parent company:
John Deere

Description

John Deere was top of the UK tractor sales league table in 2005 (the most recent figures available) with a 27.5% share of new registrations.

The popular 6020 series tractors were built in Germany and consisted of the five four-cylinder models 6120-6420 S (84-125hp), and the five six-cylinder models 6520-6920 S (121-166hp).

The medium-sized 6820 (shown) gave out 140hp and is a useful size for powering machines like the Netagco Reekie 5154 de-stoner used when preparing land for root crops, in this case carrots.

New 6030, 6030 Premium and 7030 Premium series tractors have recently replaced the older models.

21

John Deere 8530

Assembled and/or manufactured in:
USA

Parent company:
John Deere

Description

John Deere's answer to Case IH's Magnum range and other similar sized tractors is their 8030 series.

These large tractors are available in five models: the 225hp 8130, 250hp 8230, 280hp 8330, 305hp 8430, and the 330hp 8530. As well as the standard wheeled versions, the range is also available on rubber tracks as the 8030T series.

The top of the range 8530 is shown in conjunction with an Amazone Cirrus 4001 Super drill which features a two-row disc harrow unit before the seed coulters and can be used in a variety of situations and soil types.

22

John Deere 9620

Assembled and/or manufactured in:
USA

Parent company:
John Deere

Description

Until very recently the most powerful John Deere tractor available was the 9620 which sported a 12.5 litre 500hp engine under the bonnet.

Although the articulated 9020 tractors were also available on twin tracks as the 9020T series, the example shown is a wheeled 9620 equipped with John Deere's H-Trak tracked units in place of the wheels. These units could also be fitted in place of the rear wheels on conventional tractors, giving the best of both worlds.

23

Lamborghini 1306 Turbo

Assembled and/or manufactured in:

Italy

Parent company:

SDF (Same Deutz-Fahr) Group

Description

The Lamborghini tractor business was purchased by the Italian Same Group in 1972, and since then the two tractor ranges, along with Hürlimann, have been closely related.

The mid-1980s saw Lamborghini introduce a number of new models, including the 1706 Turbo which, with 165hp under the bonnet, extended the range.

A slightly smaller sister to the 1706 Turbo was the 125hp 1306 Turbo, an example of which is seen here.

More recently the colour was changed from white to silver.

24

Landini Powermaster 180

Assembled and/or manufactured in:
Italy

Parent company:
ARGO Industrial Group

Description

Landini's three-model Powermaster range was launched in 2006 and features the Italian firm's Autopowershift transmission which provides 32 forward and 24 reverse speeds. As with many modern tractors the front axle is suspended to give a smooth ride.

Similar to systems utilised by other manufacturers the Dual Power system, together with the engine electronics, gives an increase in power when the tractor is engaged in PTO work.

Shown here is the baby of the range, the 171hp Powermaster 180.

25

Description

Leyland 272 Synchro

Assembled and/or manufactured in:
UK

Tractors no longer produced

Leyland's 272 Synchro, and its four-wheel drive counterpart the 472 Synchro, were both powered by the company's own 4-cylinder engine which gave out 72hp.

The main feature of the tractors was the Synchro gearbox, providing 9 forward and 3 reverse speeds, all being full synchromesh to allow on-the-move changing, unlike previous machines.

Here a very smart 272 Synchro, fitted with the Leyland Q cab, is seen on the headland of a winter bean field with a Richard Western twin-axle trailer.

26

Marshall 802

Assembled and/or manufactured in:
UK

Tractors no longer produced

Description

In 1982 the tractor division of British Leyland was purchased by the owner of Track Marshall Ltd, and so the Leyland tractors went on to be reincarnated as Marshalls.

The 802 and its four-wheel drive sister, the 804, were both of Leyland descent and powered by 82hp turbocharged 4-cylinder engines.

The 802 shown is equipped with rear dual wheels while rolling ploughed land with a gang of Cambridge rib rolls.

The marketing of Marshall-branded wheeled tractors finally came to an end in 1991.

27

Massey Ferguson 6290

Assembled and/or manufactured in:
France

Parent company:
AGCO

Description

Massey Ferguson launched the Perkins powered 6200 series in the late 1990s to replace their outgoing 6100 tractors.

The flagship of the popular range was the 6290, and with 142hp under the bonnet it was a useful workhorse for arable tasks. This example is drilling spring oilseed rape with a 4 metre Lely power harrow and Combi-Pneumatic air drill set-up.

In 2003 Massey Ferguson introduced the 6200's replacement, the new 6400 range of tractors which also replaced the smaller models of 8200 Xtra tractors, and currently covers 95-215hp.

28

Massey Ferguson 7490

Assembled and/or manufactured in:

France

Parent company:

AGCO

Description

The Massey Ferguson 7400 tractors, launched in 2003, use the same engines as the 6400 series and consequently have the same power outputs. However, the 7400 range only includes six models with ratings from 125hp to 190hp.

Unlike the 6400 tractors which use the semi-powershift Dyna-6 gearbox, the 7400 machines feature Massey Ferguson's continuously variable transmission: the Dyna-VT.

Shown is a 175hp 7490 which is seen with a Reekie bed former re-ridging land to encourage it to dry out in preparation for potatoes.

29

Massey Ferguson 8460

Assembled and/or manufactured in:

France

Parent company:

AGCO

Description

Currently the largest tractors in the Massey Ferguson range are the imposing 8400s of which four models are available.

The range was introduced in 2005 to replace the larger models of 8200 Xtra tractors, and features SISU engines as well as the Dyna-VT continuously variable transmission.

In capable command of a 5-leg Cousins soil loosener is a 235hp 8460, busy ripping up oilseed rape stubble in preparation for wheat.

30

McCormick MC120 Power 6

Country of manufacture:
UK

Parent company:
ARGO Industrial Group

Description

McCormick's useful MC range consisted of six models ranging from 90hp to 136hp, with the first four models employing 4-cylinder Perkins engines. The two larger, and aptly named, Power 6 models made use of 6-cylinder units.

A 119hp MC120 Power 6 is seen here baling grass for silage with the aid of a New Holland BR740 round baler.

Recently, new models of MC tractors have been introduced, while the power output of the MC Power 6 tractors has changed with the introduction of BetaPower Tier 3 engines.

31

Description

McCormick MTX150

Country of manufacture:
UK

Parent company:
ARGO Industrial Group

When the current McCormick make was created in 2000 one of its first products was the MTX series which used quite a number of features and engineering know-how acquired from Case IH.

By 2002 the MTX range included six models, from the 118hp MTX120 to the flagship MTX200 which generated a maximum of 204hp.

Shown is a 152hp MTX150 planting potatoes with a Structural PM 20 planter.

The MTX range now uses BetaPower Tier 3 engines and consists of three models: the 117hp MTX120, 126.5hp MTX135, and the 133hp MTX150.

McCormick introduced their XTX tractors in 2005, replacing the three largest MTX models.

32

Description

McCormick XTX185 XtraSpeed

Country of manufacture:
UK

Parent company:
ARGO Industrial Group

One of the XTX's advantages over the previous MTX tractors was the XtraSpeed transmission which featured an eight-speed powershift, as opposed to the MTX's four, as well as the optional XtraSpeed-E with electronic range changes.

The XTX185 gave a maximum power of 173hp which increased to 198hp when carrying out PTO or transport work.

An example is shown here with a Cousins Patriot cultivator fitted with a Terracast seeder for sowing oilseed rape and other small seeds in one pass.

Recent McCormick introductions have seen the tractors replaced by the new TTX XtraSpeed series, as well as two new smaller XTX XtraSpeed models introduced (145-171 max. hp).

33

MB-trac 1000

Country of manufacture:
Germany

Tractors no longer produced

Description

The layout of the JCB Fastrac and similar machines, with the cab in the middle of the tractor allowing for a rear load platform, was nothing new.

The MB-trac was first developed in 1972 from components of the company's Unimog multipurpose vehicle.

By the mid 1980s a range of seven models was being produced, ranging from 65hp to 150hp.

In the middle of this range sat the 95hp MB-trac 1000, an example of which is seen here rowing up grass for silage with a Taarup 9084 C double rotor rake.

Production of the MB-trac came to an end in the early 1990s.

34

New Holland 7840

Country of manufacture:
UK

Parent company:
CNH (Case New Holland)

Description

In 1996 New Holland tractors were introduced as the new identity for Fiat and Ford machines.

Consequently Ford's popular 40 series tractors became the New Holland 40 series, with the same six models covering 75hp-125hp.

Shown here is a 7840, with a 100hp Ford PowerStar engine under the bonnet, on narrow row crop wheels hoeing sugar beet with a front-mounted 12-row Standen hoe.

Despite production of the 40 series finishing in the late '90s, there are still a good number to be found hard at work.

35

New Holland TM175

Country of manufacture:
UK

Parent company:
CNH (Case New Holland)

Description

New Holland's TM range of tractors included six models spanning 124-194hp. The two largest models in the range, the TM175 and TM190, used a longer wheel base than their less powerful sisters.

Seen here is a TM175, with a rated power of 177hp, working with a Maschio Aquila 6 metre power harrow breaking down land for oilseed rape.

In 2007 the new T6000 and T7000 series tractors replaced the TM range.

36

Description

New Holland T8040

Assembled and/or manufactured in:
USA

Parent company:
CNH (Case New Holland)

In 2005 New Holland introduced the T8000 range of tractors to replace the TG series. The new line-up consists of three models with rated power outputs ranging from 248hp to 303hp, provided by 8.3 litre engines.

The three tractors are all available with New Holland's 'TerraGlide' front axle suspension, or 'SuperSteer' tight turning front axle.

The most powerful T8000, the T8040, is shown hitched to an Accord MSC 6000 drill combination which is able to work in a wide range of conditions from ploughed land to 'mulch tillage'.

37

Renault Ares 640 RZ

Assembled and/or manufactured in:
France

Parent company:
Claas

Description

The mid '90s saw the introduction of the Ares range of tractors from Renault. These used Deere Power Systems engines and allowed a wide range of transmission options including Twinshift, which offered a shift under load in each gear, and the Quadrishift four-speed powershift.

A new generation of the Hydrostable cab suspension continued the Renault tradition of suspended cabs, giving excellent comfort.

Shown is an Ares 640 RZ drilling winter wheat with a Simba Horsch 4 CO cultivator drill.

38

Description

Renault Ares 836 RZ

Assembled and/or manufactured in:
France

Parent company:
Claas

Renault's successful Ares range was updated in 2002, incorporating some new features, resulting in some new models.

The Ares 800 range were the largest Ares tractors, and ranged from 156 to 194hp.

The largest Ares tractor was the 194hp 836 RZ, an example of which is seen here working down ploughed land in preparation for oilseed rape with a Väderstad Rexius Twin 450 cultivator press.

Although the Renault name disappeared on tractors after Claas purchased Renault Agriculture, the Ares name lived on.

39

Same
Antares II 110

Assembled and/or manufactured in:
Italy

Parent company:
SDF (Same Deutz-Fahr) Group

Description

In 1996 the Same-Lamborghini-Hürlimann group launched the Same Antares II tractors, as well as their Lamborghini Formula and Hürlimann Elite XB cousins.

The Antares II range was made up of the 110hp 110, shown here, and the 127hp 130, both of which utilised air-cooled engines.

The tractors replaced the previous Antares range which included the smaller Antares 100. However this wasn't included in the Antares II series.

40

Valtra T191

Assembled and/or manufactured in:
Finland

Parent company:
AGCO

Description

Valtra tractors have one unusual trick up their sleeve: they are available in a wide range of colours, the standard colours available being red, green, blue, metallic red, metallic green, metallic blue, metallic steel grey and yellow.

The latest generation of Valtra T series tractors have power outputs ranging from 139 to 211hp and feature, depending upon the specification, transport boost giving extra power when in the three highest gears, and Sigma Power which gives extra power for PTO work.

The largest tractor in the T series, the 189hp T191, is shown with a Techmagri Profilab cultivator which can be used to prepare land without ploughing.

41

Zetor Forterra 11741/4C

Assembled and/or manufactured in:
Czech Republic

Parent company:
HTC Holding

Description

Zetor tractors have a reputation for simplicity, being straight forward to operate and robust, as well as giving good value for money.

The current line-up comprises three ranges: the smaller Proxima (68-88hp) and Proxima Plus (88-109hp) tractors, and the larger Forterra models (88-128hp).

The most powerful tractor in the Forterra range is currently the 4-cylinder 11741/4C, an example of which is shown with a 3m wide Rabe MegaDrill mulch seed drill, which can be used on ploughed land or, as in this case, after stubble cultivations.

Tractor Talk

Some of the terms used throughout this book are quite specific to agricultural machinery. The following may be helpful:

Four-wheel drive — All four wheels of the vehicle are powered.

PTO — Power Take-Off shaft used for powering implements.

Powershift — Clutchless gear changes.

Some of the large parent companies and the manufacturers they own:

Parent Company	Tractor manufacturers owned
AGCO	Challenger, Fendt, Massey Ferguson, Valtra
ARGO	Landini, McCormick, Valpadana
CNH (Case New Holland)	Case IH, New Holland
SDF (Same Deutz-Fahr) Group	Deutz-Fahr, Hürlimann, Lamborghini, Same